Judi Noble and her son, Jeff Howell

Words from the Author - Dedication

The main reason I wrote this book, is for you, the reader. My desire is to give you a brief glimpse into the dark and hopeless world of the abused, but it's also my desire to offer hope. This story celebrates overcoming, and becoming. If you are abused, please know that **it is not your fault.** To those of you who are abusing, **you can change**.

All of you have one beautiful life to live. You have choices. Please let HIS courage be your strength to choose love, for yourself and for your family. If you're involved in abuse, understand that you can stop the generational cycle of violence. We are here to help. Please don't wait another moment to begin your new life.

I dedicate this book to my amazing son, Jeff Howell, and to his dad, Jim. Without either one of these men, this book would have no meaning. Jeff, I am so grateful for your life. I admire you, and your tender heart. Jim spent the latter years of his life determined to make up for the former years. Well done, Jim. You accomplished that which you set out to do. You are truly missed.

This book is also dedicated to the survivors of domestic violence, and to the people who were tragically unable to survive. You are the reason this book was written, and you are so courageous. I further dedicate this book to anyone fighting to regain their voice, dignity, and life. This is a struggle that few understand unless they have experienced it personally. I honor all of you and pray that you will no longer be afraid to stand up for the truth. I BELIEVE YOU!

Last, but certainly not least, I dedicate this book to My Lord and Savior, Jesus Christ. Without HIS unconditional love and healing, I would not have lived to write this book. He receives all of the honor and applause.

Much love to each of you,

Judi

Radical Reconciliation

A Story of Overcoming Domestic Violence

By Judi Noble

Isaiah 40:31

"Yet, the strength of those who wait with hope in the LORD will be renewed. They will soar on wings like eagles. They will run and won't become weary. They will walk and won't grow tired."

Chapter One

When I first met Jim, I was a naïve and fairly innocent thirteen-year-old girl.

I was walking home from Emerson Junior High School with my books pressed against my chest, and I felt myself growing warm under the Southern California sun. I looked up from the sidewalk and noticed a friend of mine driving a few girls home that also attended Emerson. They recognized me and stopped to ask if I wanted a ride. Flattered but unsure of the situation, I reluctantly accepted their offer. Jim was sitting in the front seat.

He was much older than I was, and had this charisma about him that I couldn't help but admire. He smiled and moved over to let me sit next to him. I reacted shyly to his gesture, and just as I sat down he quickly slid back toward the door so that I plopped right on his lap. Before I could say or do anything, he reached out and closed the car door. Red faced and completely embarrassed, I succumbed to the fact that I couldn't move or get away. I heard my girlfriends giggling in the backseat, and I feigned a giggle myself.

I was a proper Christian girl in the '60's, stuck sitting on this person's lap that I'd never met before. It was quite an unexpected predicament to be in.

As the car pulled up in front of my house, I was terrified that my mother might see me. I was forbidden to ride in a car with a boy, let alone an older boy. I darted out of the car as fast as I could and ran up to my house, but not before I heard Jim call out after me.

"Hey Judi!" he shouted.

I turned quickly and looked at him. "What?" I called back.

He flashed his blue eyes at me and paused before saying with a broad smile, "I am going to marry you someday." My heart jumped inside my chest. My head said, "*he is crazy*" but my heart said something quite different.

***

Shortly after my chance encounter with Jim, I met another boy. During this time my family situation was distant. I came from a somewhat prominent family, and while they were good to me, there was a need for us to keep up appearances.

My father was often absent due to work, but when he could he doted on me and we had a special relationship. Yet our close bond was something my mother felt threatened by, and instead of being proud to have a daughter who adored her parents equally, I sensed that she was resentful of my father and I.

This manifested over the years and drove a distance between my mother and I, and made my father reluctant to spend time with me. My mother loved me, but to this day I'm not sure she liked me.

My complicated family situation left me feeling unloved, whether it was warranted or not. Alcohol was also a factor for both of my parents, and I was often left to fend for myself. I didn't realize it then, but I was starving for a sense of family and belonging. These emotions fueled a deep, painful longing in my heart.

During this time I started discovering that my outer appearance was attracting boys around me. I was incredibly shy, but the attention was quite appealing to me. Being deprived of a strong male figure in my life left me vulnerable to almost anyone who would pay attention to me, especially young men.

This led to my complete adoration of the new boy, who was also much older than me. He picked up on my emotional cravings and quickly swept me off my feet. We assumed the title of boyfriend and girlfriend within a few months, and my desire to feel special was fulfilled.

I was still such a child. I was with this new boy often, though my parents had no idea. When they asked me where I was going I told them I was with friends. In my adolescent mind I was telling them a truth of sorts, though my fabrications kept them from knowing how much trouble I'd gotten myself into.

My childlike feelings for this boy felt like love to me, especially as I grew to depend on him. He became my family. His mother knew of our relationship and loved me, and I her. She was always happy to see me and welcomed me like a daughter. In a weird, twisted way I was getting the attention that I so craved, both from a mother figure and from a man – but it was at a great price.

The price was physical and emotional abuse, though I didn't recognize it as such. I rationalized the attacks in my young mind, telling myself *"this is probably my fault."* I didn't feel loved by my own family, at least this boy and his mother gave me the attention that I longed for, and they welcomed me.

I desperately yearned to be close to someone, so I accepted his abuse as a part of our relationship. I was young and my insecurity was blinding. I had no idea that I wasn't giving myself enough credit, nor honoring my true worth.

At 15 I had already been in a physically and emotionally damaging relationship for nearly two years. My situation led to isolation, a drop in grades, deep sadness, defiance, and the inability to leave my abusive boyfriend. The powerlessness I felt was a reality. I knew I needed to tell someone, but whom? I needed to tell my parents, but how? It would break their hearts.

Inevitably my parents found out. In an attempt to help me break free they restricted me from seeing this boy. I was so desperate for his acceptance, that I ignored their discipline. This choice caused a great deal of pain for my family and myself. Guilt and shame became my constant companion.

While it may seem surprising that young people can fall into such a pattern, 1 out of 3 teens experience abuse to this day. Young people are often vulnerable because of low self-esteem, broken families or economic hardships.

I have a great deal of empathy for young people experiencing these issues. We must find a way to raise our children with parental security and love. I believe that love can change the course of desperate children's lives. I know it would have changed the course mine. I am not looking to point blame at anyone, as I know my parents did the best they could. That doesn't change the fact that my life felt empty at times, with family dysfunction, resentment, and apathy playing major roles in my self-defeating choices.

***

I never thought I'd see Jim again but in 1963 he walked back into my life. I was a sophomore in high school, and I was still in the relationship with the boy who was abusing me. Jim immediately recognized the severity of the situation I was in. He jumped back into my world and we quickly became friends. I was desperately trying to separate from my current relationship, and Jim helped me get away from my abusive partner. He rescued me.

After Jim helped to pull me out of the abuse, we started dating. It wasn't long before my ex-boyfriend caught wind of our romance, and he became so enraged that he attacked both Jim and I in front of my house.

Jim stood up for me, and once again I felt like he'd rescued me from a volatile situation. I began to feel special, fought for and loved. I began to ask myself, *"is this what I have been looking for? Is Jim my answer?"*

I trusted Jim, and began to fall deeply in love with him. He was my hero. He provided a sense of comfort and safety, and was incredibly charming and attractive. Our chemistry was undeniable, our passion envious –for the time being.

Chapter Two

When we first started dating I still didn't fully understand how much I needed Jim to validate and affirm me. Just like my previous relationship, I used a man as my emotional barometer. If he was ok, I was ok. I became very dependent on Jim, which empowered him to behave however he saw fit.

In the beginning we embraced being silly teenagers, laughing so hard at nothing that we would literally cry and then laugh some more. This was the mood for the first several months of our relationship. We were discovering similarities. We both loved music, being with friends, dancing, and of course, being goofy.

It wasn't long before he introduced me to his parents, and they were amazing. His mother and I hit it off right away and the two of us would talk for hours. Once again I was accepted as part of a family, and I absolutely adored being with Jim.

His love for me seemed real. We were getting serious and by the third month I was sure this relationship was headed in a positive direction.

However, Jim's charms began to slowly melt away to reveal something more sinister. After I'd escaped one abusive relationship, I found myself entering into another. The abuse started subtly. I began to notice the critical jabs about my silliness, which was once mutual fun. He would become irritated easily. I noticed a change in his attitude, and tried to figure out what I had done to make our relationship change so fast.

Unfortunately, I blamed myself. About four months after we became an item, he'd started taking shots at me about my weight, my intelligence. I began to question if Jim was truly my rescuer, and my hope of finding a love that was kind and safe was once again being dashed.

He grew insensitive, putting his needs ahead of mine. He'd use words to manipulate me into believing that I was somehow undeserving of his affection, and that I was the lucky one in the relationship. Jim also had a gift for knowing how to shake my confidence. I now realize it's because he was afraid to lose me or have me seem appealing to someone else.

On one particular occasion we were out dining with friends, and I ordered my dinner. When it came to the table we were laughing and carrying on, and I had made a slight joke towards Jim –all in good fun and in the spirit of the moment.

The comment didn't sit well with Jim, and when I picked up my fork he looked at the plate and loudly said, "Are you really going to eat that? You know you're a little fat, I can't believe that's what you ordered."

There were similar situations when he would wait for prime opportunities to berate and mock me in front of our friends, which drove me into a state of silence. I stopped telling him how I felt about anything for fear of being publically ridiculed.

There were a handful of occasions when I tried to leave Jim because the verbal and emotional abuse was escalating. Yet he used his gifts of charm and manipulation to convince me that I would never find anyone else, and that no one in the world could love me like he did. I felt myself slipping away, and found it easier to let Jim make all of the decisions.

The transition from savior to assailant is common among abusers. They often swoop in to fix a person's life, only to turn around and expect something in return.

Abusers will exploit a situation to their own benefit, and make their partner believe they are not valuable without them. What so many people don't understand, myself included, is that they should never rely on their partner's opinion to determine self-worth.

Youth can sometimes cloud judgment. I was barely sixteen-years-old, and I didn't realize that it was *not* my job to make Jim happy. That his actions were his alone and that I shouldn't feel compelled to be apologetic or responsible for his behavior.

I was constantly giving, and I never asked him for anything in return. However, if I slipped up and did ask for something, it didn't go well. It was as though he constantly needed to be in control, even of my wants and desires. This should be a red flag in any relationship, for being in a relationship means reciprocating.

A person should be able to ask or require something of their partner without push back. As a young teenager, I didn't realize that this one-sided relationship was a classic warning sign for domestic violence.

What complicated my situation was that we had good times in between the bad times. Our first few months were like a dream, and even after the emotional abuse started, we would feel close and wonderful in between verbal attacks. We both found joy in music, and danced like the world was our stage. On one occasion Jim danced with me in the middle of the grocery store, much to my delight and embarrassment.

Our relationship filled my need to be loved, which at the time felt as enormous as the Grand Canyon. He wasn't ashamed of holding my hand in public or expressing his love for me, which was an issue in my previous abusive relationship.

One night we went dancing and he had packed a beautiful basket with all sorts of delicious foods. After the dancing we went to a nearby park and ate, laughed, and just enjoyed each other. These moments were the reasons I chose to stay. I loved his spontaneity, and despite the many warning signs, I once again began to believe that I had truly found my soul mate.

Chapter Three

Before the abuse turned violent, I thought I could handle it. I convinced myself that I could change him. Yet Jim's initial emotional abuse and possessiveness were only the beginning of his malice.

The first time his fist hit my face, hard, it was an absolute shock. We were riding in the car enjoying a beautiful Sunday afternoon, and the breeze was a relief. I can't recall exactly what we were discussing but I said something that obviously triggered him. The hit came out of nowhere.

Because of the abuse I had endured in my previous relationship, I was fairly adept at reading body language. I could anticipate, in most situations, when violence was about to take place. At that time Jim and I were getting along quite nicely, and I had begun to trust him. I was completely caught off guard when he threw the punch. It was the last thing I expected him to do, and I was in no way prepared for the hit.

Shaking from the blow, I fought to regain my composure and started to remember what this man rescued me from. What I had given him credit for saving me from.

Since I was physically abused for years in my prior relationship, I thought I had found my knight in shining armor with Jim. I was now struck physically and emotionally with the reality that my new hero was no different than my previous villain. Sitting there in the car, I thought to myself, "*So this is love*?" At that moment I started to believe that this is what I deserved, that this was as good as it was going to get.

My personality continued to change, and I grew more and more passive. I didn't realize it until much later, but the day he hit my face was the day my voice died.

***

When Jim asked me to marry him, I was certain this was our answer. "*Surely he wouldn't beat me if I were his wife?*" There are moments when I wish I could go back in time and ask myself what on earth I was thinking. But again, there are times when youth can cloud judgment and love can urge you to act blindly.

Taking my vows, I believed every word I spoke. My heart raced, just as it did the first time we met in the car. His words echoed in my mind, *"Judi, I am going to marry you someday."* The day had come. He kissed me tenderly and we sealed our vows to each other.

The honeymoon was fabulous.

We traveled down to San Diego and had the time of our lives. The July weather was perfect, and we laughed and loved like never before. The trip was filled with idiosyncratic gems. We discovered that the two of us should never sail without a sailor on board, and that the sun will scorch newlyweds to a deep shade of red. We relished every moment.

When we returned from the honeymoon, we found that our friends had toilet papered our tiny apartment and left gifts and well wishes everywhere. We had arrived in our new home with our lives ahead of us. I believed my dreams would come true. We could make this work. I remember thinking devoutly, *"I can make this work. I just have to watch what I say and how I say it. I will be beautiful and make him so happy."*

The next few months were well. We were both working and busy being newlyweds. I was beginning to relax, and my trust in our relationship was slowly returning. *"Could I have been right?"*

I began to think I'd been right about Jim changing after marriage, believing that he wouldn't hit or verbally abuse his wife. Unfortunately it was on our four-month anniversary that every facet of abuse I had endured up to that point returned in one night.

I had fixed a nice dinner and was waiting to enjoy a wonderful night with my new husband, but that didn't happen. Whatever upset Jim at work was about to be taken out on me. I had borrowed my grandmother's recipe from my father, and painstakingly prepared a delicious meal that I was proud of.

Jim sat down at the table, candles lit and silverware set properly. He took one bite and said, "This is disgusting!" He proceeded to become verbally abusive, telling me I was a horrible wife and lacked any sense of domestic duty or talent. He told me I was worthless.

The abusive words penetrated my heart like a knife. They seemed to implant seeds of lies about myself that I would struggle with for years afterward. The physical violence returned that night as well. I was broken hearted.

The physical abuse I received that night was horrible, however, the verbal and emotional abuse was equally as damaging. I had a sensitive heart that drastically affected my confidence as a woman.

Jim would constantly comment on my weight, and in addition to believing that I could keep him happy with my attitude, I believed I could keep him happy by staying thin. I began to engage in an eating disorder, and lumped dieting into my wifely duties. I convinced myself that if I could manage my weight and our home, I would be able to manage his happiness and he would change.

During that time we had great friends and wonderful family –though no one knew to what extent we were struggling. We had so much despite the abuse, but I realize now that what we were missing was a relationship with the Lord Jesus. At that point in time, I didn't know how to have a relationship with Him.

Life was all about working to be good enough, working to look thin enough. I had sensed Jesus many times during this era of my life but felt so inferior, and dismissed the idea that I could have a relationship with the Lord. I felt undeserving of love from anyone.

But I loved Jim, and to this day I believe he cared for me in his own way. Yet the violence continued to increase, and no matter how I behaved or what tactics I used, he continued to lash out at me.

I know now that Jim needed more help than I could offer, and that no one can force another person to welcome God's light into his or her life. I didn't realize that his compulsion for violence was a brokenness carried by him alone, though I tried so many times to fix it. It is an absolute myth that we as partners can mend our abusers alone, or make them happy.

My hope faded as the violence continued. The fear I lived with daily was incredibly painful. However, many years later I now know that out of pain comes tremendous purpose, if we let it. God will find use from our abuse, because that is who He is. He will never waste anything that happens in our lives.

Chapter Four

Early in our marriage Jim went back school, and I worked to support the two of us. One morning I was getting ready for a shift when I noticed Jim radiating hostility. As usual, this was when his negative behavior started to occur. I was incredibly careful with all of my actions and words to avoid setting him off. I referred to it as "walking on eggshells" and it's a feeling many victims are familiar with when trying to avoid abuse.

I went to work and carried on with my day. The day had been long, and Jim had arrived home earlier than me. When I returned our house was a disaster area. A kind, loving partner would have been sensitive to the fact that I put in nine hours of work and would have pitched in to pick up our mess.

Instead, Jim was livid that the house wasn't clean. My intuition from earlier that morning had been correct, and my efforts to tip toe around Jim's hostility were in vain.

Abusers often consider their partners objects that exist only to fulfill their needs. At that moment, he needed an organized environment. I started picking up trash off the floor, trying to hide my irritation and fatigue.

I reached down to grab another item off the floor when Jim smacked me in the face so hard it sent my flying across the room.

I was dumbfounded, hurt, and enraged. I stormed out of the door, slipped into my car and drove away with no particular destination in mind. Silent tears rolled down my face as I wondered if our relationship would ever be different. Would I always be driving away from him in fear, with eyes black and blue and constant tears that I felt would never cease? I was losing hope.

When I returned a few hours later, the house was spotless. Flowers sat atop our coffee table as dinner simmered on the stove. Jim walked in and professed his unending love for me, and swore it would never happen again. He said he was "sorry" and that he never meant to hurt me. Yet after his apology he slipped in a comment. He said that if the house were clean in the first place, none of this would have happened. He was indirectly blaming me for his behavior.

This episode is a prime example of the Cycle of Violence. The first step in the Cycle of Violence is tension building. Anxiety fills the air and victims do anything possible to calm the abuser, which is what I attempted to do the morning of this incident.

Step two of the cycle is abuse. It should be noted that abuse comes in more forms than physical. This includes emotional, sexual, and psychological mistreatment.

Step three is where the apologies come in. This is one of the main reasons the abused "stay." A thousand thoughts can run through victims' minds following apologies, "*Maybe he will change? Maybe this will be the last time? I don't want to leave. I want to make this work. For the time being, things will be ok.*"

When victims receive long awaited attention during step three, they experience what feels like true affection. These are the crumbs they digest to feel emotionally satisfied. The abuser will buy gifts, expensive dinners, and go out of his way to make the victim believe it was the last time abuse will happen.

Step three also deals with blame. Even though the abuser will often apologize, they will insinuate that the abuse wouldn't happen if the victim didn't provoke them.

My experience with Jim was not the first time I had entered into the Cycle of Violence, and it certainly wasn't my last.

Chapter Five

When I made the decision to leave Jim, it was out of pure necessity. I had to be safe.

At the time I was working days at a pediatrics office. When I wasn't at work I was at home with Jim, and we were living with another couple. It was a strained living situation, but having other people around helped keep the violence to a minimum. Yet Jim would still find a way to exert his authority over me, and I would end up on the receiving end of physical and emotional abuse.

After accepting that our marriage had become too dangerous for me to stay, I left him in the summer of 1969. I was thankful for my job, and for my co-workers at the pediatrics office who had become my support system. I remember thanking God for that job because I believed (and still believe to this day) that my steady paycheck and supportive friends were the blessing that made my escape seem possible.

All too often victims feel tied to their situation because of controlled finances or the lack of a job.

The abuser will convince the victim that they can't afford to leave. They will use economic abuse as a tactic to make their partner stay, withholding funds, cash, credit cards or child support.

I instinctually decided to leave Jim quietly, and stay with a friend for a few days. Leaving a relationship is the most dangerous time for abused women and men. Why is escape the most dangerous time for a victim of abuse? Because the one who is abusing realizes they no longer have the ability to control, manipulate or exert power of the victim.

To the abuser, their partner is a drug – an anesthesia if you will. When there's a chance the drug will be taken away, most addicts will fight to the death to get their fix. It's no different when an abuser is about to lose control of their partner, essentially losing their drug.

The decision to leave quietly was vital to my escape, and because Jim had so much control over my life, leaving quietly allowed me to exit. If victims try to reason with an abuser, they seldom end up leaving. If I had confronted Jim, I never would have escaped.

I left when I knew had an opportunity to be safe. Luckily I had a friend in town to turn to until I could figure out a permanent living situation, and to this day am grateful to her for taking me in.

It wasn't long after I had left Jim that I started to experience strange symptoms. I was constantly fatigued and noticed that I had gained weight, particularly around the midsection. Then it hit me: *Could I be pregnant?*

Yes. I could.

When I found out that I was pregnant it was the happiest day of my life. All of the months I had spent at the pediatrics office marveling at all of God's little wonders had made me yearn desperately for a child of my own. And now, I had a baby growing inside of me and I felt special. My child felt special.

I remember being so excited that I ran out and bought a blue set of pajamas because I had convinced myself that I was carrying a boy. I couldn't wipe the grin off my face. The excitement and joy rushed over me, and I was helpless to believe that this is what Jim needed to change. A dangerous hope had crept inside me that this child meant that our marriage could be saved after all.

The urge to tell him increased and I found myself daydreaming about what it would be like to give him the news. It was almost as if I had imagined a romantic movie replacing our relationship.

I envisioned myself bursting through the door with a handful of balloons and telling Jim that he would be a father, and he would wrap me in his arms and be a changed man forever. The balloons would fly into the air and we would laugh at how great our life was about to be.

I told my friend in town that I wouldn't need to stay with her any longer, and that Jim and I were going to work out our troubles and start over. I still get emotional when I remember how naïve I was, and weep at my willingness to compromise my baby and my safety.

Chapter Six

When Jim and I were still together, we'd had a false alarm. I remember telling Jim that I thought I was pregnant, and for the most part, he seemed excited. I knew he wanted a child but his reaction had traces of fear, and I knew it was because of our problematic marriage.

The week after I found out I was pregnant, I planned my visit to Jim's. Still hoping for my romantic fairytale, I even stopped for a half a dozen colorful balloons. As I walked up to the door, my heart raced with excitement. This time it wasn't a false alarm. As I raised my hand to knock on the door, I took a breath. "*Maybe I'll just walk in.*"

Walking inside I could hear Jim's voice from upstairs. I assumed he was on the phone. A feeling of uneasiness swept over me instantly, though at the time I couldn't explain why. Before putting too much thought into it, I picked up the telephone downstairs to listen in on his conversation. When I heard the other voice on the line I began shaking violently –it was Jim's high school girlfriend.

I carefully replaced the phone on the receiver. I could have run out of the door. I could have left all my anger in that apartment and walked away. But I didn't, and I let my emotions get the better of me.

I ran up the stone stairs, my feet pounding hard against the dense stairwell. I ran into his room, balloons still in hand, and saw him lying on the bed with the phone to his ear. The balloons slipped slowly from my grasp as I saw the look on Jim's face. My anger swelled and I screamed at him, "You will never see your child!"

I felt betrayed. He wasn't fighting for me, or for us. He was in a relationship with someone else. He was making no effort to change himself or devise a way to win me back. When I picked up that phone all my fears had become a reality, but more than that, my heart was completely broken.

I guess I had always questioned if Jim really loved me, and hearing him talk to another woman validated my suspicions. It was true. He didn't love me. Walking up the staircase, the only thing I wanted to do was confront him. To make him understand that I had come to forgive him and start over, and he had ruined it. I never for moment thought of how badly this might play out for our unborn child or for myself.

Upon hearing the reproach and anger in my voice, Jim snapped. A look crossed his face while he was still lying on the bed that I had seen before and it horrified me. He didn't believe I was pregnant, and was convinced I was manipulating him. Anticipating what was coming, I rushed to leave.

Before I could get out of the door he jumped up and grabbed me by my waist-length hair. He twisted me to the ground and proceeded to drag me down the stone stairs. Every step sent shock waves of pain throughout my body.

Once he pulled me to the bottom, he turned around and began kicking me in the stomach. His malice hit my abdomen over and over again. He was kicking me as hard as he could. I was finally able to pull my knees into my stomach, instinctually protecting my unborn child. He then aimed his kicks at my shins.

After he'd grown tired of attacking me, Jim dragged me out the door onto the front steps and left me there. I lay there for a few minutes, unable to move and convinced that if I did he would come after me again. Because I had experienced Jim's rage before, I knew that any movement I made might grab his attention. The unfortunate reality is that I could anticipate his behavior when it came to abuse. He would attack me then walk away, and oftentimes come back with more violence.

Laid out on the porch, it was almost as if time was suspended. I realized how badly I was injured, and tried to pull myself together.

Laying there on the stoop, I prayed harder than I ever had in my entire life. I prayed for our unborn child, for God to save him. I cried and pleaded with the Lord to save this innocent baby. Something chided me to stand, and I slowly rolled to my side as best as my injured body would allow. I believe that God had heard my prayers, and gave me the strength to move and attempt to get up.

I could feel the severity of my injuries. I could barely stand, and I did my best to pull myself upright. I began to place one foot in front of the other, and like a child learning to walk, had to find my center of gravity. I adapted to my injuries and started to hobble toward my car, each step shooting unbearable pain through my shins and abdomen.

From behind me I heard the door open. My heart stopped and in a moment I knew what was about to happen. He was coming back for more.

There's an old adage that states that when a baby is stuck under a car, a mother can draw superhuman strength from adrenaline and lift the vehicle to save her child. I believe the second I heard the screen door my body's instinct to survive came alive, and I knew I had to run.

I could hear Jim's quick footsteps pursuing me, and I prayed to God to help find the strength to move quickly. Tears streaming down my face and sounds of agony escaping my lips, I ran away from what I considered to be my certain death. I jumped in the car and slammed the door shut with Jim's hand still inside. I drove away with it stuck there out of for fear of my life.

Chapter Seven

To this day I'm not sure how his hand made its way out of the car door as I drove away, but I later found out that the damage wasn't permanent.

After I left Jim's I fled to a friend's house that I worked with at the pediatrics office. I was so frightened and riddled with anxiety that it took me hours to calm down, but once I did we headed straight to the hospital.

The examination revealed that my baby was fine. There are no words that can accurately describe my elation when I learned that my child was going to be okay. Once I had registered the baby's well being, I had time to process my own emotions. I was devastated. Yet I was determined.

No matter what, I knew that this time the relationship was over. No more going back and believing Jim's words of "I'm sorry" and "it will never happen again."

That was the last beating I would take, and the last one that my baby would ever endure.

Betrayal can only be felt if the perpetrator is someone you genuinely care about. God help me, I loved Jim. Yet that love didn't change our situation, and in that moment I knew that he was toxic to my life, and that I had to protect my unborn son.

I was determined to build a better life for my child. I had been working at the pediatrics office since I was eighteen, and at this point I was twenty-one. I was incredibly grateful for my employment, and throughout the years the folks in the office had become my family. God had set me up perfectly with this job.

Before the confrontation with Jim about my pregnancy, I was in complete denial about our future. I had told the friend that I was staying with originally not to expect me back. I was certain when I left her house to speak to Jim that day, my fairy tale romance would come true and we would reconcile. This blindness is common for people who are abused. Finally leaving him was like coming out of a dark cave, and it was a cave I had been in for years.

It felt like I had left the darkness, squinting my eyes and attempting to focus on the reality of what was really happening. I was incredibly confused, as well as being terribly frightened of the future. I was so accustomed to being controlled and told what to do that I'd forgotten how to make my own decisions.

I sought out advice from my family, and though I know they loved me, my parents considered Jim dangerous. When I spoke to my father about what was happening, he hugged me and told me he loved me. He went on to tell me that the strained relationship I had with my mother was an issue, and that I couldn't come home.

I had no idea what to do, or how to take a step forward. The first decision I did make after the beating was to go somewhere that Jim would never find me. I checked myself into a motel located near my work.

Though I had a wonderful day job, I didn't have much money when I fled. I spoke with the motel manager and began working nights as the switchboard operator to pay for my room and board. Again, I felt that God was with me. Yet during this time I felt immense shame.

Now that I'm older, and have helped hundreds of women flee similar situations, I find it so strange that anyone who has suffered abuse would feel shame. There is no logical reason. They--we--are the victims. But nonetheless during that time I felt like I was a failure.

At the motel I spent many nights wondering what other women in my situation would do. I was fortunate that I could barter work for room and board. Yet what about women who didn't have that opportunity? Where would they go? Who would keep them safe? There was a moment when I actually said out loud, "If only I could create some sort of place where women like me could go."

I was homeless, and as that truth dawned on me, I was horrified. "Where do women like me go?" I asked the air, or God, or anyone who would listen. The terrible truth about homelessness is that close to 67% of women who are currently living on couches, in backrooms, motels, cars, and on the streets, are there due to domestic violence.

These thoughts at the motel were so important to my life, and to my calling. I know that God hated what was happening to me, but he knew the enemy would not win. During those days a dream was born in my heart, and for the first time I heard my calling. God trusted I would listen. However, the painful journey was far from over. My husband was determined to be in my life. It was tormenting.

Chapter Eight

Audrey, my friend from the pediatrics office who drove me to the hospital, eventually found I had been living in a motel for nearly two months. She insisted that I move in with her, her husband, and their three daughters. They were so hospitable to me. I have to admit that I was embarrassed at how well they took of care of me, but in the end I embraced it and knew how fortunate I was to have them.

I was a part of their family for several months. Audrey was a wonderful mother and extended her maternal grace to me, and was my friend and confidant. She also helped me understand how important it was to take care of myself, and shared her nursing knowledge with me several times.

She was also a source of strength, and even though Jim was trying to find out where I was, I knew I was safe. I could count on Audrey.

One evening I was leaving work, very pregnant and very uncomfortable.

As I was walking out I saw a figure out of the corner of my eye, and I had a sense of alarm though I didn't understand why.

Then I saw him. Jim was standing by his car waiting for me. I froze with fear. He saw the terror in my eyes and immediately tried to calm me.

"Don't be afraid," he said. "I promise not to hurt you." He had made that promise before.

It was still daylight and my coworkers were inside so I felt that I could I answer him. Very cautious, I kept my distance and asked what he wanted. His eyes were watering and he looked shocked. "You really are pregnant?" he asked. "I thought you were lying to save our marriage."

I was so angry at that moment I wanted to scream, but knew better. To my amazement, he stood there and cried. I had heard rumors that Jim was saying that if I was pregnant, the baby wasn't his. Now I knew they were true.

Out of anger I said to him in a deeply sarcastic tone, "Well, you don't have to worry about it now do you? Since this child is not yours!"

As I spoke I wondered why I was being so sarcastic. So much hurt and anger poured out of my heart. I should never have given him the time of day, let alone risk setting him off. As I walked away Jim called out, "I deserved that Judi. I know this child is mine."

I couldn't hide my tears, and I turned to him and said, "It's too bad you didn't realize this earlier. It's a little late for tears and I will not subject this baby to your rage."

I realize now that taking that step to protect my child was the first step in finding my voice again.

I got in the car and waited with the doors locked until he left. This was before cell phones, and in today's technologically driven climate I'd advise women in similar situations to call the police. But there I was, in the 70's, pregnant and locked in my car for safety.

After he had left I went back into the office where I collapsed in Audrey's arms. I was safe. I realize now, years later, that I was struggling with Post Traumatic Stress Disorder (PTSD). Many domestic violence victims suffer with the same. It's debilitating at best.

Looking back, I wish I could have known what was happening to me. The fear, the hypervigilance, insomnia, depression, panic and sadness are incredibly hard to deal with when you're trying to put your life back together.

Today, I run a non-profit organization called Eagle's Wings Ministries that's dedicated to victims of domestic abuse. I encounter women on a daily basis who are suffering from PTSD. This is a serious condition that needs to be treated with medical attention. There is help, and there is hope.

***

Life was good leading up to the birth of my child -- for the most part. "Single mother" wasn't a title I'd had on my dream list, but I was strong and I was surviving. During the divorce I had made an important and empowering choice to withhold the fact that I was pregnant from the courts. The decision was difficult. It meant I would be raising our baby without Jim's financial assistance.

However, I was very aware of the law. If I shared the news of my pregnancy I would be forced to share custody with a man that I felt was dangerous to both my baby and myself. I wanted to completely separate myself from Jim to keep him away from our child; custody was not an option.

It's an odd thing coming out of an abusive relationship. You don't stop loving that person. I still loved Jim, but I started to let all of his good qualities go and accepted that he had demons I couldn't battle for him. I loved my unborn child so very much and I knew Jim was far too abusive to let him anywhere near our precious baby.

My heart grew strong and I knew I had to protect him. This meant choosing to raise him alone, and that was what I wanted and needed to do. And while all of these revelations were becoming clear, something else started to happen. I began to love and value myself. I continued to find my voice.

Jeffery came into the world at a whopping 8lbs 14 oz on April 26th 1970. He was perfect, and my heart was full. This boy was meant to be born. I had overcome so much, and knew we had an amazing journey ahead.

God had given me an incredible gift in this child. His big, blue eyes, his dimples, his smile. Everything about him would light up my heart and light up a room, and still does to this day. I felt like the adventure was just beginning, and what an adventure we would have.

One of the many amazing gifts I received from God after I'd left Jim is that I had the great relief of knowing that all of my little family's medical expenses would be covered, and for a single mom, that was truly a blessing. My job enabled not only the medical care that I needed, but provided me with diapers, formula, immunizations, and even stitches. Many, many stitches.

Chapter Nine

Jeff was a wonderful baby. I had an instinctual feeling that he had a destiny to fulfill, and God had entrusted me to help bring that destiny to life. I had never felt such joy in my life. Holding that little bundle in my arms, bringing him to our home for the first time, it was a dream come true. This little life was already making such a huge difference in so many others. He made me smile constantly, and I realized that I had never known true joy before Jeff.

The first few months I hardly slept because I would check on him every hour. I was happy to do it, and felt incredibly blessed to get to know him. He was a happy baby, smiling and giggling all of the time. I remember reading to him, and he would look up at me with those huge blue eyes like he understood every word I was saying. It was just the two of us, and it was wonderful.

I dreaded going back to work, but I was the breadwinner. I wanted it that way. I didn't want Jim anywhere near this precious little life.

He didn't pay child support because of the decision to withhold my pregnancy from the courts. God would provide what we needed, and I swore to myself that Jeff would not be subjected to abuse.

The inevitable day came when I had to return to work. Searching for a babysitter was grueling, because I felt that no one was good enough. I finally settled on a woman who ran a service out of her home and had three kids of her own.

Leaving Jeff for the first time was terrible. I felt like someone had stabbed me right in my heart. This little boy who I adored, who I had fought for, who I had protected, was now staying with a stranger. This was the life of a single mother.

Every day after work I would rush to the sitter's to get Jeff as soon as possible. One day, when he was about seven months old, I came to pick him up early. I walked up to the house, and there in the front yard was my babysitter watering her lawn. I waved, naturally, and as she looked up and saw me her face fell to complete horror.

Dropping the hose, she ran inside the house and I was on her heels. She quickly darted for the bathroom and was nervously telling me that she was only outside for a moment. I stalked behind her into the bathroom and there was Jeff. Alone. In the bathtub. Livid doesn't even begin to describe how I was feeling. I scooped Jeff up and we never went back.

The hunt for a new babysitter was on. In the mean time, I had recruited every trusted friend I knew to watch Jeff until I could get someone who would care for him properly. I was still working at the Pediatrics office, and was always running into amazing families. On one particular day there was a woman in one of the rooms with seven kids. They were all taking with her at once, and she seemed delighted to have the conversations. I chuckled to myself as I thought, "*This is the most patient women I have ever seen*." My next thought was, "*she must babysit."*

I asked her if the children were hers or if she was babysitting. She said four of the children were her own, three were in her care, and four more of her own were at home.

"Wow! Incredible! Do you have room for one more?" I asked. Without hesitation she said yes, and we agreed that she would start watching Jeff the following day.

Even though I had just met this woman, my instincts told me that I had found Jeff's long-term caregiver. My instincts turned out to be correct. Geri Kidd and her husband Larry have been a part of my family's life for the last forty-five years. My little Jeff quickly became a "Kid Kidd" and Geri is still a close friend to this day.

As a mother, knowing your child is taken care of is a wonderful relief. Yet Geri was more than that, she was a person I could turn to for advice, and someone who always had an open ear and an open heart. I was truly blessed to find her. She called me with first steps, new words, and new feats Jeff would accomplish. I am so forever grateful for God's provision for us through this family. My babysitter took my child in as her own, and adopted me along with Jeff. I quickly became a beautiful part of this family.

Chapter Ten

In 1971 my faith had grown. I had declared my love for the Lord publically, which was a huge step for me. My heart felt softer. I felt different, and I knew I was loved. Even though I had ignited a new bond with the Lord, I was a very young believer and had much to learn.

Jesus was the One that I had been waiting for. Yet more than me waiting for Him, He was waiting for me. I will be ever so grateful to the Lord for fighting for me with such a pursuing love.

When you love someone, as I had loved Jim, you feel extreme betrayal when you suffer abuse. Naturally, I had grown bitter towards him. Forgiveness was never a part of the plan –until I met Pastor Keith Korstjens.

When Pastor Korstjens suggested I get baptized I was a little unsure, as I had already been baptized as a baby.

Pastor Korstjens countered, "I'm sure you were, now you have the wonderful opportunity to know what it feels like to be totally washed of your ugly past and sins, and to be completely forgiven."

He asked me many questions about my life and my past. There was much that I was ashamed of, and it was difficult to have this conversation. I was not kind when I told him about Jim, and even less kind when I shared that Jim and his new wife were expecting a baby. I began to sob, and all of the pain Jim had caused was surfacing.

Pastor Korstjens was incredibly comforting as he listened to my story and replied with words of support and prayer. I hadn't discussed what had happened with Jim in so long. It was difficult, yet liberating to have this conversation. However, nothing could prepare me for what he was about to say next.

He looked at me with kind eyes and said, "Forgive."

Through my tears was a face of disbelief. Forgive Jim? No way. He didn't deserve forgiveness. I hated him. After a long pause Pastor Korstjens looked me directly in the eye and said, "Judi, do you want to spread anger, hatred and bitterness to Jeff? You will if you don't do something soon. You are so full of hate right now."

I couldn't believe it. How could I be so transparent? If he could see my anger, Jeff could too, but I still felt that Jim didn't deserve my forgiveness.

"I can't," I told him. "He doesn't deserve it."

He replied, "I know he doesn't. But this isn't about Jim. It's about you."

Pastor Korstjens went on to share the concept of forgiveness as a whole, and questioned whether or not any of us deserved to be forgiven. He reminded me that God sent his only Son to die for our sins, and that he lived his life to teach forgiveness and spread love. It was still a hard concept to accept. So much had happened, but deep down I knew he was right. I was still holding on to so much anger, hurt, and bitterness.

"I don't want Jeff to become bitter and angry like me," I said, still struggling to keep my composure. "But I don't know if I can forget everything that's happened."

"Judi, I'd never ask you to do that," he said. "And neither would God."

He went on to explain that forgiving Jim meant releasing him to God, and reassured me I would never have to see him again if I didn't want to. Forgiving him was about letting the pain go, and moving on. Not forgetting, but moving forward. That day in Pastor Korstjen's office, God began to soften my heart even more.

CS Lewis states, "Unforgiveness is the poison we drink to kill someone else."

It was literally starting to destroy me. That day was a game changer for me. I was no longer giving any more of my power, or my life away. Complete forgiveness took years but I knew I was free. I will be forever grateful to Pastor Korstjens for his amazing influence in my life.

We don't want to become what we hate. Harboring bitterness will turn you into someone you no longer recognize, and while forgiveness is a process that can take years or decades, it's an act that will set you free. It's a way to let go, not a way to forget. When I took a step toward forgiving Jim, it was the first step in a very long process. Sometimes anger will help you flee from abuse, but once you're safe victims owe it to themselves to let go of the hatred that can consume your heart. Making room for forgiveness is actually a way to dispose of the hate.

To be clear, forgiveness does not mean being nice to your former abuser, or letting them back into your life. Instead, it's a way to move forward.

Chapter Eleven

Starting to forgive Jim was a life altering experience. The process took endurance, but I realized that I was changing for the better. I began to let the bitterness go. I was becoming a better mother, friend, and employee. My sense of humor began to return and I felt joy rushing into parts of my life that had gone dormant. In short: I felt like I was waking up.

Jim was with his new wife, and I no longer felt like he was a threat to me. Beyond that, I felt stronger. I felt like I could handle more on my own. Looking back at what Jeff and I went through and how we survived makes me proud to this day.

It wasn't always ideal, but we loved our way through everything. I was taking care of Jeff, and I was blossoming into a person that I always knew I had wanted to be.

I was grateful for this newfound strength, and it carried me through several situations. Jim would drift into our lives every so often, but I felt capable and mature, and confident that I would make good decisions.

One particular Christmas Jim stopped by our little duplex. Jeff was two-and-a-half, and playing in our front room. When I opened the door, Jim stood there with a gift in his hands. I was shocked, on the defensive, but most of all confused.

This was the first time the three of us had ever been alone together. When he asked if he could come in, I hesitated. After a deep breath and a prayer I motioned for him to come inside. I need to explain that there are many women who are put into this same situation, and don't experience what I did.

Men that are abusive are manipulative creatures that can charm their way into many situations. They should be treated with extreme caution, and as a general rule, shouldn't be allowed into your home. For me, I made the decision to let Jim in. I was fortunate.

When he walked in Jeff ran up to him and wrapped his arms around his father's legs. Jim was taken aback, and dumbfounded. Whatever he had imagined taking place, this definitely wasn't it. He looked down at the little stranger who was a piece of him and said, "Well, hi there."

Awkward doesn't begin to describe the atmosphere. Jim was unsure of how to behave around Jeff, and even more uncertain how to behave around me. When Jim handed Jeff the Christmas present he opened it with two-year-old abandon and was immediately impressed with this stranger who had brought him a gift. They began playing together, and my heart broke.

I'd always wished things could have been different for my Jeffery. That he could have had the father he deserved. Witnessing the immediate bond between the two of them was difficult. They looked so much alike, and they both smiled genuinely at one another.

Jim turned to me with tears in his eyes and whispered, "He's so smart."

I replied, "Yes he is."

I felt my anger returning in that moment. Again, forgiveness is a process. I thought to myself, *"Why doesn't he just admit what jerk he is? Why can't he realize what he's missing? Why can't he get help and try to win my trust so I'd let him begin to be a father?"*

When he left the duplex that day, Jeff looked up at me and said, "Where is Daddy going, Mommy?"

I lost it. How could he possibly know that man was his father? No one had said a word. I bent down and picked Jeff up and hugged him for several minutes. I couldn't help but cry. Jeff was such a sweet boy, he cradled my face in his tiny hands and said, "Don't be sad, Mommy."

Back to square one where forgiveness was concerned.

That day I discovered that you can love and hate in the same moment. I would have done anything for Jim and Jeff to have a healthy relationship, yet there was no way I was ready to trust him, and I wasn't going to push it. I think that deep down I knew he wasn't ready. It broke my heart, and years later I would learn that it broke his too.

Chapter Twelve

During Jeff's childhood I continued to work at the pediatrics office, and life was good. I had Geri, and I had friends and family who I could count on. My faith grew stronger, as did my self-confidence.

Several months went by and we didn't see or hear from Jim. Though he had been out of the picture for some time, I still kept in touch with his parents. They were kind and supportive of me from the beginning. They were also good to Jeff, and had earned my trust. I would often let Jeff visit with them, and I was grateful for the relationship. That was the only tie to Jim that I had.

I continued to attend church with Pastor Korstjens, and began building a life for myself that allowed room for empowerment and healing. People often say God doesn't give you more than you can handle, and I believe that this time of personal growth was for a purpose.

One afternoon I was attending church when I saw Jim. He walked in with his beautiful new wife, and she was very obviously pregnant.

I was completely unprepared. He had stepped into my comfort zone, a place where I felt safe and loved. It's disabling to be caught off guard like that, yet there I was quivering on my own turf. I was certain it was another manipulation tactic.

My impulse was to yell. I wanted him out of there. Abused women suffer psychological scars as well as physical, and I wasn't mentally prepared to deal with this situation. I went to my head Pastor, Dr. Ted Cole. Pastor Korstjens was the associate Pastor and assured me that Dr. Ted (as he was fondly known) would hear my heart. I pleaded with him to ask them to leave. There were a hundred churches that Jim could have walked into, yet he chose mine. My emotions were running high, and I was convinced Jim's only mission was to manipulate me into letting our families become acquainted. Whether this was true or not, I was not ready for this to happen.

Dr. Ted was sympathetic, but he was also logical. He asked, "Judi, do you know why he's here? A small boy drowned in his neighborhood. They're here to be with his family who comes here. Jim and his wife are their neighbors."

I heard the words that he was saying, but they weren't registering. My heart broke for this poor child's family, but I was still convinced Jim had shown up as a control tactic. It was too much. Dr. Ted recognized this, and proceeded to ask Jim and his family to leave.

Making this request was empowering for me. It was important for me to use my voice and take care of Jeff, first and foremost. Dr. Ted's decision is an important part of my journey for two reasons. The first being that I realized how much power Jim still had over me. The second being that for the first time in years, I felt vindicated and defended. Dr. Ted was like a true father and hero in that moment, because up until then no one had stood up to Jim in front of me. I had spoken up, and it had made a difference.

Chapter Thirteen

After the encounter with Jim at the church, I moved forward on my path of healing and empowerment. My life was about to take a turn that would require every piece of strength I had worked for.

It was a beautiful, cool day in December of 1974. Jeff was four and had already started kindergarten, but he was home with me on a break. I was busy putting away Christmas decorations while he was playing with a pack of friends, and I put on music while I cleaned. Bob Dylan came on, singing a lyric about "dying young." I stopped in my tracks.

Life's a funny thing, sometimes the most obscure moments will cause you to stop and acknowledge something that you've been avoiding. That's what Dylan's lyrics did to me, and I finally admitted to myself what I'd been trying so hard to ignore.

I had been feeling sick for about two months. Hearing the song made me think back to six months ago when I had felt a small pea sized lump in my right breast.

At the time I had told myself I'd wait a month and check it again, but life rushed ahead and I rushed with it. After all, at twenty-five I was too young to have breast cancer.

At this point I had already completed training to become a Licensed Vocational Nurse, thanks to my Grandpa Stadler, who had helped support me while I was in school. My Grandma Palmer had also been an incredible source of support, and I credit her to this day for helping me understand that women can be full of strength – and I would soon need more strength than I could have imagined

As a nurse, my logical side had told me to keep an eye on the lump. As a mother, time had flown by. I realized on that December morning that I couldn't ignore my symptoms, and checked the area again. I froze.

"Could this really be the same little lump?" I thought to myself. *"Dear God, help me. It's the size of a golf ball."*

A rush of memories came flooding back as I remembered how much time I had taken off of work because I just didn't feel well. I felt like I had the flu on and off for months, but still didn't add it all up. *"Oh no. Is it Cancer?"*

I was twenty-five years old and terrified that I had cancer. And Jeff, what about my precious boy? It was more than I could handle.

I called Audrey and she came right over. I had her check the lump hoping that I was overreacting. When she felt it her face went pale with fear and her eyes began tearing up. I knew I was in trouble.

***

I had found the lump over the weekend. When Monday finally rolled around I called my doctor's office as soon as it opened, and they asked that I come in as soon as possible. Audrey, being an RN, had called in a favor to schedule an immediate appointment to check the lump. Everything was going so fast I felt like it was spinning out of control. Meanwhile, I was in complete denial.

When I arrived at the doctor's office we proceeded with a mammogram. The metal plates were cold against my breast and a thousand "what ifs" swam through my mind. It was the 70's and mammograms very new and a bit archaic. I had dense breast tissue and the test couldn't pick up the tumor. When my doctor shared the news I could tell he was trying to be upbeat, but the seemingly positive results were not resonating well with either one of us.

"You have a couple of options," the doctor shared. "You can wait six months and we can recheck you, or you can do a biopsy."

I sensed a strong "No" forming in the back of my throat in response to waiting six months. In fact, I felt the Lord telling me, very clearly, to get the biopsy and have it taken out. My spiritual side, my instinctual side, and my maternal side were all screaming to have the lump checked –and removed.

My thoughts naturally turned to Jeff, this little life I had known for such a short time. I left the room, and in that moment, the cry of a mother's travail escaped my lips. I sobbed before the Lord, "*Please don't take me now.*"

The biopsy was scheduled for January 8th at the Pomona Community Hospital. I went in for the test surrounded by friends, and when I came out of the biopsy they were there to greet me with kind words and flowers. When the anesthesia wore off and I had fully regained my senses I immediately asked for the results, thinking they would be available.

"What's the news?" I asked my friends and family who had gathered.

They all told me to wait for the doctor, and frustration washed over me. Everyone in the room was either praying for me, or reading the Bible. It wasn't doing much to calm my fears, and if I'm being honest, the scent of all of the flowers reminded me of funeral. The sun began to set and finally the doctor came in. I remember the doctor's quiet, serious voice as if it were yesterday.

"Malignant, grade four carcinoma with four out of nine nodes infected," he said.

"Prognosis?" I asked.

He replied, "We can't say. Let's give it time."

Chapter Fourteen

When the diagnosis was revealed, I felt like someone had punched me. They recommended a modified radical mastectomy with radiation and two years of chemotherapy. The mastectomy would be done the following morning.

The doctors had been so certain that the tumor was benign they didn't even have me sign a release for a mastectomy. And there we were, less than twenty-four hours later, preparing for surgery. My first reaction was quiet panic that turned into anger. I looked at the faces staring back at me from the hospital room and screamed, "Why didn't one of you warn me? Not one of you had the courage to tell me for seven hours?"

When I am afraid, I will oftentimes get angry as a coping mechanism. All of the people gathered in the hospital meant well. My boyfriend at the time was in the room and the look on his face showed that he likely felt the worst. He just didn't know what to do.

I asked a few more questions, and then cried. We all cried. I had six people on my bed, crying with me. That was the exact comfort that I needed, and to this day I'm incredibly grateful for those friends.

When everyone left, I spent some time with Audrey and we talked about the future. "What about Jeff? What about my job? What will I look like with only one breast? How do I accept the fact that I must lose a body part in order to live?" Audrey just listened patiently.

There was no plastic reconstruction in those days. The surgeons were after a cure. I was grateful for that, but so devastated at the loss of a part of my femininity. I was, once again, questioning my identity.

I never left the hospital after the biopsy. The surgery went forward as scheduled the following day. It all seemed to happen so quickly. I awoke early that morning and went into the bathroom. I dropped my hospital gown and stared at myself, at the body that I had been so hard on.

"You are not thin enough, tall enough, tan enough, big breasted enough..." The pain in my heart welled up in my throat as I began to realize that this would be the last morning that I would ever see myself the way God made me.

I shook with sobs. I went to the floor and prayed as I cried, "*Oh Lord, how did I get here? Am I really going to lose my breast at 25? Maybe even my life?*"

I drew strength and told myself, "*Yes, I can do this. Yes, I will do anything to live. I must live to stay alive for Jeffery. I will not let anyone else raise this child.*"

An orderly had come into the room to take me into surgery. I had showered and pulled myself together as much as I could. He helped me onto the gurney, and thus began the long ride to the OR. I was trying not to cry, but the tears were rolling down my face.

I was looking up at all the lights on the ceiling and was actually looking forward to being put under, even if it was to have my breast removed. "*Why had my body turned against me?*" As we entered into the surgery room the orderly did the strangest, sweetest thing. He spoke, almost as if he could read my mind.

After he handed me a tissue he bent down and kissed my forehead and said, "Don't worry Judi, you are going to be alright."

I was so touched by his kindness. I asked him what his name was and he said Jonathan. I said to him, "Thank you Jonathan, you will never know how much your words mean to me."

He smiled and left, and the room began to slowly fade as the anesthesia set in.

***

I had told my friends and family not to come the next day. I needed time to be by myself. I wanted to be left alone. The pain was far beyond anything I could have imagined. I was heavily sedated, but the level of discomfort made it impossible for me to rest. Despite my request for my friends to stay away, they slowly trickled in. Monte, Audrey, Joan, and a few others went against my wishes, and it was wonderful. The prayers began and the pain lessened.

When I became more coherent, I asked the charge nurse if I could get a message to the orderly, Jonathan, to thank him again for his kindness. I described him to the nurse and she emphatically said, "We do not have any orderly by that name or that even remotely looks like what you have described."

Now that I am a bit older in the Lord, I realize that He sends angels to help us when we are in need.

Psalm 91 verse 11 & 12 reads, *"For he will command his angels concerning you, to guard you in all your ways; they will lift you up in their hands, so that you will not strike your foot against a stone."*

What a sweet angel Jonathan was.

Chapter Fifteen

I spent nine long days in the hospital and my precious boy was being cared for by my mother, and then by his caregiver, Geri. I missed him so much. People came to see me and didn't know what to do or say.

Being diagnosed with cancer is so surreal. All of a sudden I was totally aware that I wasn't invincible. Life was fragile and I would not live forever. When you're young "tomorrow" is something you take for granted. I had always assumed "tomorrow" would be there.

I had requested that Jeff not come to see me in the hospital. It was one of the most difficult decisions of my life, but I felt it was the right thing to do. After being away for nearly ten days, I was finally released to go home. I was anticipating seeing my boy, and I had only been home a few hours when I received a call from Jeff's kindergarten teacher.

He had run away from school to look for me. Bless his little heart, he'd had enough. My heart broke! I could just imagine him walking home by himself. He was an incredibly brave child, but in that moment I was an anxiety-filled mom. It was a long way home and he was so little.

I instantly got out of my bed and hobbled to my car, hoping it would start after sitting in my driveway for well over a week. It did, and with tears in my eyes, I set out to find my Jeff. As I drove I felt relieved that I could see the streets, the trees, the stores. I had survived to see all of these wonderfully familiar sights. I slowed down as I saw a little boy carrying his lunchbox, walking with strong steps.

I parked in the street and called out to him, "Jeff!"

He turned, "Mommy?"

Too weak to pick him up, I sat down on the ground and gave him huge hugs and kisses. "I missed you and I am so sorry that I had to leave you, I won't ever do that again!" I wept as tears streamed down my face and I rocked him back and forth. It was at that moment that I knew Jesus had answered my prayer and that I would be healed. Jesus had given me the gift of courage through this child – the will to live and the strength to fight, and to fight hard.

Chapter Sixteen

In 1986 I had been cancer free over a decade. Through Jesus, I had defeated my death sentence.

When you experience something like that, you come out differently on the other side. Life feels different. I had acquired a sense of appreciation that wasn't completely visible to me before. I opened my eyes enough to thank God not only for my son, friends, and family, but to thank him for myself. I was a survivor in many ways, and I was grateful of that fact.

When Jeff was sixteen, I was full of joy. My son had grown into a loving, confident young man. I was healthy, and I had a job in a doctor's office at the nearby hospital. I felt that everything I'd gone through, from abuse to cancer, had made me stronger. Because Jim's parents were still a part of Jeff's life, I knew that my former father-in-law had fallen ill.

Since he was being seen in the hospital, I decided to swing by his room to wish him well and check on his status.

Once again I would need to draw upon the strength that I worked so hard to build up.

I have to admit the thought of Jim being at his father's bedside should have crossed my mind. Perhaps it was the busy nature of the day or maybe time had caused me to be less cautious about running into my ex-husband. Whatever the reason for my lapse in vigilance, it didn't change the fact that I was completely caught off guard when I saw Jim sitting in his father's room.

When he saw me he almost looked relieved, like somehow he had been hoping I would stop by. Despite his seemingly genuine smile, I immediately tensed and became very aware of my surroundings. He rose and blurted out, "Judi!" and then started toward the doorway with his arms outstretched in anticipation of an embrace.

At that moment, something escaped from me. It was a feeling that surged through my entire body in the span of a second, and lifted me up. I opened my mouth and the words, "You will not touch me!" crossed my lips with force. More than twenty years after meeting Jim, I had finally found my voice.

Initially he looked shocked, but his expression of shock quickly gave way to sorrow. I turned on my heel and headed out the door. He chased after me, begging me for a moment of my time. He pleaded with me, and when he said, "Please, Judi! I want to see Jeff!" I stopped in my tracks. I asked God for guidance and turned to face him.

"You will never see him."

Jim refused to give up. He was in no way disrespectful, but he was indeed persistent. After many requests I finally agreed to have a conversation with him after work. I was reluctant, but he convinced me to allow my only son to spend an afternoon with his father. I made it very clear that if Jim slipped up in any miniscule way, he would never see Jeff again. From there, Jim made good on his promise. Every time Jeff was with his dad I could see a difference in him. He was happier. He looked forward to his time with Jim. They were growing closer --I had to keep my fears in check.

Jeff shared their experiences with me and there was a day when he told me, "Mom, I know Dad isn't perfect, but who is? I need to form my own opinion about him. He's good to me, Mom."

My son was becoming his own person with his own ideas. I was so impressed. Through all the hardships that he had endured without a father, Jeff was making discoveries about life and himself through Jim. Fathers have an amazing ability and strength to call out the gold in their children. I believe it is a power that is given to them by our ultimate father, God.

Today, we live in such a fatherless generation. We need fathers to be involved and help raise their boys to be kind, yet strong. We need fathers to set an example for their daughters and to show them what good men are like.

The years went by, and to my surprise, Jim poured his heart and soul into gaining trust from both Jeff and myself. It wasn't easy, but I finally accepted that Jim wanted to be a part of our son's life, and that Jeff was welcoming the change. I had spent so many years longing for my son to have a father, but never trusted Jim with the privilege. Now, after so many years, Jim was stepping up to the plate and Jeff was flourishing.

Chapter Seventeen

Jim and Jeff's relationship continued to grow over time, and I started to see changes in Jim for the better. Jeff decided that he wanted to go to San Diego State University, and so he did. He put himself through college, and did so with very little help from me. I have to admit it was incredibly difficult to let him go, however, I was also in a place where I could start allowing time for myself. Seeing my son happy and thriving somehow made space for my own desires, and my thoughts kept drifting back to my time in the motel.

The thoughts were more like echoes, really. Welcome whispers that circled around me, reminding me of how blessed I was to stumble across that little motel. In a time where I had nowhere to go, nowhere to escape to, I found a place that Jim would never find me.

I could work for room and board. This is not a common situation for women fleeing domestic violence, largely because of control and economic abuse.

While these thoughts were coming back to me I was thriving. I was working in orthopedic sales and embracing a new sort of independence. I loved that job, and it gave me freedom and finances all at the same time. I decided to take a trip to Alaska to see my dear friend Karen and it turned out to be the adventure of a lifetime.

Karen had lived in Alaska most of her life, but we had met each other in junior high school. Her father lived in Southern California, and she was staying with him for a year when we met in school. I am so grateful that God wove her into my life. We have quite a history.

I hadn't seen her in years, and it was a gift to be with her in beautiful Alaska. I had accepted Christ when Jeff was a baby, privately, and Karen was the one who led me to the Lord at that time. She was, and is, very special to me.

We fished, hiked, and took in God's glorious northern landscape. One afternoon we were fishing on a riverbank when I took a moment to lie down and enjoy the beautiful blue sky. I had stretched out my legs and rested my hands behind my head, and peered upward.

That's when a verse came to me. I heard Isaiah 40:31:

"Yet, the strength of those who wait with hope in the LORD will be renewed. They will soar on wings like eagles. They will run and won't become weary. They will walk and won't grow tired."

It came on so strongly that I sat upright and whispered, "What?"

The response was loud and clear. *"This will be the name of your ministry and this will be the verse that it will live by."*

"Lord," I responded. "What will be the name of the ministry? Wait, what ministry?" The word left my mouth before I had even realized it.

His response was just as loud as the first. *"Eagle's Wings will be the name. Yes, this will be the ministry that I placed on your heart years ago. Love my girls, Judi. Love them and tell them how much I love them. Tell them, Judi. Tell them."*

By this time I was crying and Karen rushed over to check on me. I could barely talk, I was so overcome with joy and anticipation.

I realized why those echoes from the motel were circling around me. Why my wishes for women to have a place to go had found me once again. In that moment on the riverbed, God's gift of that verse had led me to my calling. I knew that my wish to start an organization for women must be turned into a reality, and that I would call it Eagle's Wings. My pain was becoming His purpose.

I believe that people can have spiritual connections to places. I believe that Alaska, for me, is one of those places. I felt at peace there, and my heart had finally opened wide enough to hear my life's calling. Twenty-five years after my time in the motel room I knew how I could help women similar to me. Eagle's Wings was officially born in November of 1995.

I returned from my trip and obtained my non-profit status, and began funneling my years of experience ministering to abused women into my own organization. I obtained my official domestic violence coaching certification and Eagle's Wings became legally incorporated. We started small.

***

A year later I returned to Alaska, and affirmation found me once again. My friends and I had left the airport and headed to Cook's Inlet, a quaint, but beautiful, cove.

Walking up around the bay, I heard a startling noise from above. I looked up and saw a family of eagles sitting side by side. The father was breathtaking, with a wingspan that must have stretched seven feet. The mother was alongside the baby and we all stood there, captivated. The baby eagle suddenly flew away, and the mother immediately flew after her baby. That's when the father let out a screech that pierced the sky. The mother and infant eagle turned and joined the father, and the three of them flew off together into the distance.

I took that experience to heart, and considered those majestic creatures a sign. I believed that what I had witnessed meant that a man would be coming into my life very soon. At the time I was a bit giddy because I thought that man would be a new husband, but alas, God had something quite different in store for me.

Chapter Eighteen

There's no single way to define love. There's no handbook, and certainly no rules. When I fell in love with Jim all those years ago, it was purely and deeply. We had many good times, and to this day I hold on to those memories. To be clear, there's no excuse or rationalization for abusive behavior. No person should ever endure domestic violence, which is why I've dedicated my life to helping survivors. However, it's important to acknowledge that there are times when people can change.

This is a difficult concept to express, especially for me as I have witnessed many horrific situations in my years as a domestic violence advocate. The truth is that it's extremely difficult for abusers to change. It requires humility and repentance that is deeply felt. Responsibility must be taken for ALL of the abuse, and blaming the victim must be stopped.

Yet there are instances when abusers embark on the long journey to reformation, and every so often succeed. This is what we pray for. The heart beat of Eagle's Wing's lies in family reconciliation, whenever possible.

But first and foremost, we are committed to keeping the abused from harm. We never, in any way, suggest that a person return to a home or situation where violence is a factor.

In 1998 Eagle's Wings was helping small numbers of women, but I didn't have the reach I'd hoped for. I continued to work and help the families that needed me, but I was also working many hours as a saleswoman. One afternoon I received a phone call from Jim's third wife, Carol. He had been divorced from his previous wife for some time, and at this point I had respectful relationships with both of them. In fact I was fond of them.

"Judi hello, how are you?" Carol said from the phone.

Her motive for calling me had caught me off guard. She was reaching out to invite me over for a visit. I was hesitant, yet over time I began attending family functions for Jeff's sake, and it was worth it.

It was difficult for me as I really didn't know my place as the ex-wife, but Carol was so cordial that it made it a bit easier to interact with Jim and Jeff's side of the family.

My visits were often brief, but they were friendly. In all honesty, Carol was incredible. I look back at this time as a total miracle. We had learned to love without jealousy or comparison: two women who adored their families, and wanted to share in Jeff's life.

As time went on Carol and I began praying together. We knew that Jim and the kids needed our love and prayer, and we had become sisters of sorts in our mission. We both wanted Jim to find the Lord. He was kind to Carol, and undergone a great amount of growth. I would later find out that with her help, Jim had agreed to attend a seminar called "Breakthrough." That seminar was about to change many, many lives.

***

In 2001 I received a phone call from Jim. It wasn't the first time I'd spoken to him over the phone, and I wasn't expecting anything out of the ordinary. Yet before I could even say hello, I heard sobbing. He couldn't speak, but I still knew it was him.

"Jim! Jim what's wrong? Is it Carol? Oh Lord, is it Jeff?"

He spoke in between sobs, "Please, please Judi, forgive me."

Those words resonated through my entire body. People often talk about time standing still. I'd never given the expression much thought, but in that moment, time did indeed stand still. I began to sob.

He continued, "I don't know how you could even talk to me. I don't know how you could ever forgive me."

Jim had spent the weekend at the "Breakthrough" seminar, where a very effective coach had made quite an impact on Jim. For four days he had gotten in Jim's face about his choices, and largely about his choices concerning myself and his ex-wife, Linda. I'd come to find out that this coach was relentless, and wouldn't give Jim any room for excuses. He had gotten through to him, and Jim finally understood what he had put us through.

From over the phone I heard him repent. It was legitimate. There was no mention of "I'm sorry." Instead it was words from a man who got it. He realized the severity of his behavior, and with that poured thirty years of pain. He accepted responsibility for his actions, and admitted that he was completely in the wrong. Every time. No exceptions.

We spoke over the phone for the next two hours. We cried together, and we shed decades of bitterness and disdain.

"I'm coming over," he said.

"What? Why?" I asked in disbelief.

"I have something, I need to give it to you personally," he said. His voice was still shaking.

When he knocked on my door I almost didn't recognize him. His face was puffy from crying, but more than that, his demeanor had changed. I invited him in and he handed me a letter that was clutched in his hand. It was a letter of commitment. I read the letter while it shook in my hand, and I looked up at Jim and knew this was the moment when our relationship changed.

We had undergone a radical reconciliation.

What we experienced is rare, but I pray that anyone hoping for the same change in their abuser could know what this feels like. That they could witness their abuser undergo reconciliation with those who they harmed.

It took a great deal of humility on my part as well, as I let go and repented for years of hate and bitterness. That day we changed generations. There would be no more abuse in our family. We changed the course of our family's future, and their families to come. Love had finally won.

Jim had found the Lord in a way I never thought possible, but more importantly, the Lord found him. True forgiveness between us had begun. Freedom had found its way into our lives. It was an amazing beginning to a whole new radically reconciled relationship.

After that day I watched his life for the next six months. We kept up over the phone, and after that six-month span both he and his wife joined the board of directors for Eagle's Wings. This may sound unbelievable, and it should. Jim was in the minority.

He had found the grace of God and dedicated the remainder of his days to living a life that he could be proud of. Together we started the "Love Does No Harm" seminars that still operate to this day. These seminars welcomed both the abused and the abusers, which is a controversial practice that has earned Eagle's Wings both praise and scorn over the years.

Though it was rare, abusers did attend the "Love Does No Harm" seminars. Jim and I decided that if they were willing to come forward, we were willing to treat them. When Jim and I were running the seminars together he was magnificent. He knew how to handle the abusers. He could see through their lies, their fears, and their pain. He was bold. He would call out their behavior, and challenge them to change their ways.

I am grateful to this day for his tremendous work with these men. They needed another man to love them, yet strongly call them on their abusive behavior. For many of these men, Jim had become a spiritual father.

We witnessed a small handful of families reconcile because of these important workshops, and many more found the strength to escape abuse and enter into independent freedom.

Through all of his deep struggles with anger and pain, Jim had found a way to positively affect people. He finally understood the concept of responsibility, and had found a way to change.

It should be noted that our "Love Does No Harm" seminars were carried out under my watchful eye, and Jim was open to my suggestions. He appreciated my advice when dealing with people who suffered from domestic violence, and often looked to me for guidance during the seminars. There was incredible restoration in our relationship, with monumental changes that were apparent in both of us.

My heart was finally beginning to heal, and I had begun to soften. I was grateful to the Lord for helping me accept Jim's repentance, and for having such a strong presence in both of our lives.

To be clear, Eagle Wing's top priority is the safety of the abused. We stand by those who have lost their voice to a violent partner and need support. We align with people whose lives are altered from physical, emotional, and financial abuse.

Reconciliation is a long road, and requires a strong support system for everyone involved. I have seen so many cases where the abuser wants to change, believes he can change, but chooses not to. Before anyone attempts reconciliation, they should reach out to someone with a great deal of experience counseling people who've endured domestic violence. Don't pursue this road alone.

***

Jim was an inspiration to both men and women in our "Love Does No Harm" seminars. He was proof that it was possible, and gave hope to people who wanted change. As one who had taken responsibility for his actions, Jim would stand in repentance for every man that harmed and abused the women in the room.

He would tell the women in attendance how amazing they were, how they deserved to be treated with respect. He would repent for their abusers and plead with them to start loving themselves. When Jim spoke, attendance would triple.

Chapter Nineteen

When I reflect on the course of my life, I feel overwhelmingly grateful for all of the people that I have crossed paths with. I have met so many beautiful souls who have helped me along the way, and consider myself blessed to have had the support of such wonderful family and friends. Despite the traumatic period with Jim, which was inexcusable, he was an integral part of my journey.

We created a son who is the joy of my life to this day. Jeff is married with a wonderful wife, and I am so proud of him. I know his father shared my pride. Jim and I were fortunate enough to forge a new, rare friendship.

That friendship enabled us to embark on a healing journey with Eagle's Wings, and together we positively affected hundreds of women, men, and children. I am blessed to be the Director of Eagle's Wings, and to have the opportunity to help people in need. I know that in the end, Jim felt the same.

He passed away in 2009.

When he died, I grieved with tears that had been stored for a lifetime. He was my childhood sweetheart, and the first man to truly steal my heart. We had walked a violent, difficult journey together, yet in the end, it all came back to love.

We loved each other. Not "in love" but in a friendship way that was full of laughter, teasing, harassing each other, and finding time to just reminisce of what was and what could have been. He had once again made his way into my heart, but this time he was my brother in the Lord.

He had transformed into a father that his four children could be truly proud of, and he loved them deeply. All of his children became close, and to this day maintain a tight bond and loving relationship.

At the time of his death he left behind three wonderful grandchildren. He achieved what many consider to be impossible. I believe that the "good Jim" was always there, he just didn't know how to connect with that part of himself. After decades of anger and wasted energy, he woke up. As rare as this experience is, for Jim, it was authentic. He repented for his sins and dedicated his life to repairing what he had broken.

The latter part of his life is a tribute to God and all that Jim prayed for. Please take the time to read his incredible letter of commitment on page 109. I thank the Lord for his life and legacy.

***

This year marks the 20th anniversary for Eagle's Wings. We continue to advocate for families suffering from physical, emotional, and sexual abuse. We provide hotel vouchers for emergency shelter and offer counseling and coaching twenty-four hours a day. Our "Love Does No Harm" support group persists to this day.

We've initiated our own adopt-a-family program that aids families throughout Southern California, and arrange safe houses for people fleeing violent situations. We provide assistance with legal services and attorney fees, and have access to a network of therapists, coaches, and caregivers.

One particular woman that we welcomed into Eagle's Wings was the victim of heinous abuse. Her life was threatened; she was kept captive in her own home, and was emotionally and physically abused. She came to us and allowed Eagle's Wings to direct her out of the relationship.

We hid her and gave her a place to stay, and supported her throughout her years-long journey of escaping her abuser. She is now in school to become a social worker, and advocates on behalf of Eagle's Wings. Her testimony is on page 105.

***

In my thirty years of experience I have witnessed so many people struggle with domestic violence. It is my lifelong goal to reach as many women, men, and children as I possibly can.

During my journey I've become a Certified Executive Coach specializing in Domestic Violence, and earned my Domestic Violence Advocacy Certificate to participate in legal proceedings and enter the jail or prison systems. I'm also a certified counselor, seasoned public speaker, author, and guest instructor on college campuses. Everything I've worked for up to this point has made me stronger, wiser, and has fueled my fire to fight domestic violence.

For the people reading this book who are suffering from domestic violence, please know there are people who care. There is never an excuse for abuse, and God would never ask you to stay in a dangerous relationship. God's love is endless. There are resources available and there are opportunities to change. There is room for strength, confidence, courage and love. Believe me, I know. Most of all, there is hope.

Testimony of An Eagle's Wings Survivor
(The name has been changed)

My name is Jane, and I am a survivor of domestic violence. Like many other women and men, I found myself involved in an abusive relationship for 16 years. My relationship wasn't the typical husband/wife relationship. I was involved in a homosexual relationship and was being abused by my partner. Like many relationships, the first year was great. But as time went on she began to be very controlling and manipulative. She would call and text throughout the day, continuously, checking on me and seeing when I would be home and where I was.

If I didn't answer her right away she would text me again and again until I responded. When I did she would be upset or angry that it took me so long. I told myself she does this because she loves me and is worried about me. I now realize that is not love, but power and control.

After having been together about three years we had one of our biggest arguments. We began yelling at each other and she started to slam doors, throw things and then disappeared for a few minutes only to come out with a loaded gun and pointed it at my head.

As she was yelling and waving the gun in my face, I felt myself go totally numb. I sat down on the couch and I literally could not speak. She continued to threaten not only my life, but her own. I truly thought that was the day I was going to die.

On that day, I no longer had a voice and she had complete control of the relationship. Fear was my constant companion and I just found myself isolated and losing hope that things would ever get better. For the next thirteen years I lived in constant fear of her and fear that she would take my life. I was so full of shame and guilt from this secret life style I was living that I felt there was no one I could talk to or ask for help.

In 2009 I was invited to an Eagles Wings event and that was a day that changed my life forever. It was Valentine's Day and God showed up with His love and forgiveness for me. I made a decision that day that I was going to follow Christ and gave my life to Him. I left that day knowing I was not the same person, and that I had been forgiven. I began to see Judi each week for coaching and in time I was able to tell her about my partner. I was blind to the fact that I was living in abuse until God began to show me, through the coaching.

About a year later I knew it was time to leave her and get out of the abuse, this was the scariest time of my life. With the support of Eagle's Wings I was able to tell my partner that the relationship was over and once again she became extremely angry and began to threaten my life. In 2012 Eagles Wings helped me get out and placed me in a safe house where I am currently still living.

For the next two years I began to go through deep healing and suffered from severe PTSD and depression. I became very suicidal and was having a hard time just functioning. Eagle's Wings connected me with Jana Chatham for counseling and I began to see her weekly. I also went through an out patient treatment program that taught me new tools on how to deal with PTSD and depression. I began to clearly see God working in my life. He was there every step of the desert journey that I was walking. I thank Him that I had the support of many who were loving me and praying for me.

I began to realize that I truly do have a voice, and it's powerful. I also learned that I can make decisions for myself. I began learning how to take care of myself such as grocery shopping, cooking, and buying my own clothes. The truth is that I became so dependent on her for everything that I couldn't care for myself. Amazingly, I now am able to dream again and have visions and goals for my life. One of my dreams is to finish my Bachelor's degree in social work and this past year I have had the opportunity to go back to school and work on my degree. I will graduate next year and I am looking forward to what God has planned for me.

Walking closely with the Lord Jesus for the last several years, He has changed my heart and my identity. I have chosen to no longer participate in the lifestyle I was once living. That was entirely my own decision. I know that I am HIS daughter and I am worthy of HIS love. I am completely humbled by His grace and mercy.

I am grateful to God, and Eagles Wings. My life will never be the same. I have a new future ahead of me, full of joy and living in peace.

Jim's Testimony and Commitment Letter

We were high school sweethearts, and married shortly after Judi graduated. The abuse had started before we married but escalated rapidly afterwards. When she found out she was pregnant, she left me and filed for divorce.

I began to form a relationship with my son, Jeff, during his teen years. That bond has grown into an unbelievable father-son relationship. Because of that relationship, and the desire from both Judi and I to co-parent, some communication was opened up between the two of us as parental figures. I believed that I had come to a place of repentance in regards to the abusive way I had treated her during our marriage. On several occasions, I had asked her to forgive me. Her response was always "Yes" but the feeling I got was "I will never trust you."

In 2001, I attended a 4-day experiential workshop that focused on the way we "do" relationships.

During that weekend I became very clear (heart clear—not head clear), for the first time, about the impact that my actions had on other people.

The low expectations I had for my life came from a sense of insecurity fostered by the seeds planted years before in the area of abuse and my half-hearted ownership for those actions. By the end of the weekend I was totally committed to changing my relationships, primarily (I thought) with my current wife and four children.

I wrote and presented a commitment statement to each of them speaking of promise into a real, transparent and authentic relationship. I openly confessed that I wanted "them to know that I knew" there were wounds on their hearts and their souls that were totally my responsibility, and that I would do whatever it took to help heal those wounds. I asked my wife, Carol, and both of my former wives, Judi and Linda (my 2nd wife and mother of two children and a recipient of my abuse) to hold me accountable to my commitment.

Upon asking Judi for her commitment to hold me accountable and expressing my ownership and sorrow for the way I had treated her so many years ago, both of us completely broke down. There seemed to be a closure of the past and reconciliation for the future—it was one of the most freeing moments of my life.

Shortly after this Judi asked Carol and I if we would consider serving on the board of directors of Eagle's Wings and help take a message of the hope for family reconciliation and restoration to the abused. We agreed and we started planning the workshop known as "Love Does No Harm." The vision of the workshop was to provide a safe place to explore abuse prevention through education. The first two workshops were great successes and a weekly women's "open door" group formed at The Water of Life Church in Fontana [California] to provide support for abused women in different stages of transition. This group has been and is still going strong for more than three years. A great woman of God that had attended the first workshop now facilitates it.

As we have continued doing these workshops, they have somewhat changed. Though they are still predominantly attended by women there are also more men, both from a place of abuse and also abusers wanting something better for themselves and their families. I see so much healing coming from these workshops it blows my mind.

The workshops provide an environment of safety, education, options and hope for the abused. They provide the same for the perpetrators of abuse without judgment or condemnation.

Personally, I have influence. I will open my life and those experiences anytime and anywhere in order to protect the abused or help the abuser to understand the impact of his or her actions, and for both to move into a place of healing. I believe, because of my personal experience, that reconciliation can happen. That the children of abuse can understand that it is not their fault and that they are created in love and by love. For me, an abusive relationship is an unacceptable legacy for the generations to come.

The Father Heart of God governs this work. His heart shows up every time a workshop is done along with the love and compassion of Jesus and the wisdom and guidance of the Holy Spirit. Without the Grace of God, this story would not have happened and the work would not be going forward.

In His Hands,

Jim Howell

Words of Gratitude

Thank you, Heidi Darby, for gifting me with your amazing ability to help me write my heart. Thank you for the hours and love that you invested in making this book possible. I am forever grateful for your dedication and commitment.

Thank you, Dr. Scott Lee, for never giving up me or on this book. Your friendship is invaluable to me and I thank you for your prayers daily, for both my book and the survivors of domestic violence.

I'd like to thank my dear friends Cindy, Teri, Mindy, Darlene, Joan, Monte, and so many others. You are wonderful.

Pam Havlick, my encouraging friend. Thank you for holding me accountable to finishing what I started so long ago. "Radical Reconciliation" is here, in part because of you.

To my dear friend Sue Jackson, who is now with the Lord. I love you and I know you are celebrating this book in Heaven with the ONE who inspired it.

To my parents, I love you and am so grateful for you. Though we had our ups and downs, our love prevailed. I cherish both of you.

Thank you, most of all, Lord Jesus.

Praise For Radical Reconciliation

"Martin Luther King Jr. said 'Love is the only force capable of transforming an enemy into a friend.' In your hands is a book that will lead you patiently, truthfully and graciously on this path to personal and family transformation. This is a story of reconciliation that speaks not out of theory, but out of real life experience. May you, the reader, be transformed by the grace and power of radical reconciliation as can only be shared and understood by one who has experienced such a transformation."

~Words from Pastor Fraser Venter, Lead Pastor, Cucamonga Christian Fellowship

"I would wholeheartedly recommend this book. Judi's story is one of abuse and healing. It opens a window into a tragic and challenging world that deserves our attention and understanding."

~Words from Dr. Rhonda Beckwith, LMFT, Director of Foothill Counseling Center and Associate Pastor at Foothill Community Church

"Judi's book, 'Radical Reconciliation' is one of those books that you simply can't put down. Judi shares with brutal honesty the details of what victims of domestic violence experience. She reveals the personal devastation that domestic violence can bring.

However, this story is much more than that. It is a book about incredible hope despite tremendous challenge and victorious reconciliation that only God can bring. More than simply providing a happy ending, Judi's story reveals the truth about how love conquers all. My life has been forever changed by this courageous testimony and I am certain the same will be true for you."

~Words from Scott W. Lee, Medical Director Medtronic & Clinical Professor Loma Linda University Medical Center